"THE CHERRYVELLY CH̲

TALKING PROPER

A Guide to the Art of Ulster Posh

by

Doreen McBride and Billy Simpson

FOREWORD

by Mrs. Egnes Johnston, member of the Board of Governors of Cherryvelly Ecedemy of Speech end Dramer; treasurer of Cherryvelly Dremetic Society; end Medem Chairmen of the Berry Menelow Fen Club (Cherryvelly chepter.)

Whin Ay wis esked till recommend this book Ay hed reservations because frenkly Ay don't know whit these two could possibly know about proper speaking. Mr. Simpson is some kind of newspaper chep who comes from North Entrim and this lady Doreen McBride lives in Benbridge. Hordly a recommendation. But ay allowed thim till tape some of may telephone conversations with may sister Sendra because they promised till make a donation to the Egnes Johnston Support

Egnes Hairiot Johnston

Group for Women who kin't come till terms with Enderson & McAuley's closing down.

End of course if it helps disedventaged readers till learn to talk proper then Ay wish thim the best of luck. But as for this Simpson end McBride, Ay know nothing about thur beckground end kerrecter. They don't hev any femily in Cherryvelly or Ay would know everything about thim.

Sincerely
Egnes Hairiot Johnston

INTRODUCTION

by Billy Simpson

Cherryvelly is not a geographical location and shouldn't be confused with that respectable and down to earth suburb in Belfast known as Cherryvalley.

If Cherryvelly is anywhere, it is everywhere. It is an idea rather than a place. An aspiration. A pretention if you like. It is our telephone voice. Our Sunday-go-to-Meeting clothes. Our respectable front parlour where we put the Vicar when he calls. Our job interview suit. All of us have affectations of some kind or another. Who is to say that the Cherryvelly syndrome is worse than any other?

During the course of our researches Doreen McBride and I had the opportunity for an audience with Mrs. Egnes Johnston, a central figure in Cherryvelly society. We found her a gracious hostess (although putting down newspaper for us to stand on and plastic sheets over the chairs before we were allowed to sit, might be thought a 'tad extreme' anywhere but Cherryvelly.)

She agreed to bless our enterprise since she felt "Perheps it's time to help the pore pethetic folk who don't live in Cherryvelly, till be able to speak as if they did."

Talking with mouth open – sign of common folk

3

She produced her old school textbook from Eshleigh where her Tutor had written "Only common people talk with their mouths open."

"Ay hed till write thet out a hundred times one efternoon," she said, smiling fondly at the memory. "It taught me thet to speak Cherryvelly you hev till hold your mouth as if you were going till whistle. Then just talk through the wee gep in the middle."

"When youse kin do thet," she informed us, "you'll be able to pess yourselves off as a better kless of person."

The difficult part of this book, analysing the spread of the Cherryvelly Syndrome to all arts and parts of the land and explaining the social implications, has fallen to Doreen McBride. The easy part, transcribing tapes of Cherryvellyese, has fallen to me.

To achieve the best value from this book it is useful to read sections of it aloud to yourself or others since it is important to practise not only the sound but the rhythm of Cherryvelly speak.

And as Mrs Johnston so perceptively observed. "Thet wee book of yours would be the ideal gift for Ulster people living abroad who heven't heard people talk proper since they went till live in places where nobody speaks English. Like Keneda, Australia, Emerrica - end Lunding."

INTRODUCTION

by Doreen McBride

People in Norn Iron speak the most wonderful English ever invented, as described in my locally best selling book, "Speakin' Norn Iron as She Shud be Spoke." However, some people suffer a desire to be upwardly mobile and become a local type of yuppie or muppie, referred to throughout the remainder of this work as UMINIES (Upwardly Mobile In Norn Iron).

This book is intended for those who feel socially disadvantaged and wish to change their behaviour and speech patterns to join the upper crust, known locally as 'the Cherryvelly set'. They want, in local parlance, 'til larn til spak praper'. It should also help strangers and those from Cherryvelly to communicate with the common or garden Norn Iron speaker.

I am eternally grateful to Egnes Hairiot Johnston for her guidance in the preparation of this work.

We are surrounded by common people

5

TALKING PROPER

by Doreen McBride

I remember as a small child dressing in my Sunday best and calling for a friend to go to a Christmas party. My friend opened the door. I hardly recognised her. She had changed out of her grubby old jeans into a party frock. Her unruly hair was combed and tied back in ribbons and her face was so clean it looked as if it had been polished. She was delighted with her appearance. "Don't I clean up lovely?" she questioned. Her mother popped up as if from nowhere. Looked at Jean with pride, smiled, hit her a hefty wallop on the backside and warned, "Mind yew talk proper!" It spoiled the party for me. How do I "talk proper?" I wondered. I was unusually silent.

Back home I asked my mother "How do I talk proper?"

"Well," she replied, "for a start, don't say any bad words."

That is still good advice. Most Cherryvelley types are death on swear words. This makes life particularly difficult for young UMINIS educated at what could be considered socially disadvantaged schools where, in order to fit in and avoid being bullied, one has to learn to swear like a trooper.

UMINIS have an entirely different set of standards to the type my grandmother referred to as 'the arsacrockery', namely those born into an elevated position, such as people with

Don't I clean up lovely?

6

inherited titles. People of this ilk feel confident with no need for concern. They do and say what they like. The upwardly mobile must be seen to be impressive. They must 'talk proper' so swearing is out. So is any mention of homosexuality.

The general attitude in Norn Iron leaves a lot to be desired regarding political correctness. The only type of sexual relationship tolerated is that of the firmly heterosexual. An exception to the general rule is among those commonly described as being 'arty-farty', who have well paid jobs, often in the media, the theatre and so on or who have established a reputation as an artist selling exorbitantly priced works of art. This type of person is regarded as slightly different from normal mortals and is given a fool's pardon, especially if they appear to have made a lot of money. Money talks. However, the general rule among UMINIS is that homosexuality is not tolerated. Even the common or garden Norn Iron speakers who have no intention of rising and going anywhere, apart from the pub, have been known to mutter darkly, "If Ah thought he wus one av 'em Ah'd giv 'im a gud kik up the crigs." (TRANSLATION: If I believed he had homosexual tendencies I would damage his testicles.)

The upwardly mobile must be seen and heard to have stricter attitudes than ordinary workers so homosexuality is out. Give faint, small squeals of disgust or, sniff in a disapproving fashion, at the merest suspicion of what should be referred to as 'unneturel prectises'. Say things such as "Thet is deesgusstin'!" "Et is egenst the lews of netur."

I remember being in the Grand Opera House in Belfast watching a performance of the ballet "A Midsummer Night's Dream". The curtains opened revealing a spectacular set with wonderful, strangely shaped bushes. As the music progressed parts of the bushes began to move. Silver bodies climbed out of them and began rolling around on the floor. The elderly man in front of me appeared very interested. He was obviously a dirty old Norn Iron man who had been bullied into accompanying his wife as a birthday treat. "Maggie, Ah didn't think bally wud be lik thon," he proclaimed loudly, "If Ah'd knew Ah'd hav cum before this. Thons like Beaver Park on a Saturday afternoon. They shud hav a sign saying, Beware av the bush fruits!"

The young woman sitting next to me became very agitated. She turned towards me, her numerous gold chains and rings gleaming in the dim light. "Es thet quaite naice?" she asked anxiously. "Ef Ay thought they wor doing unneturel things Ay'd leave emmede-etly."

"I haven't a baldy notion," I replied, "It's ballet."

"Ooooohhh!" she sighed in relief, "Et's belly!" She settled back comforted as she knew watching ballet is socially acceptable, even if like us, one is occupying the cheapest seats. In this case make a virtue of necessity by proclaiming loudly, "Derling, one hes ei much better view here then in the stells or cercle. One cen see the dencers feet", which has the effect of letting everyone know that the individual is more interested in the performance than in being seen and that he/she normally occupies the most expensive seats. This ploy may also be used for musical productions. Just exclaim loudly "The ecoustics ore sooooo much better here then down below."

Sex is a difficult subject for the upwardly mobile. Under the age of approximately 30 years high status is achieved by having it regularly, preferably with someone rich, or famous, or good looking (or better still, all three!)

After the first flush of youth a subtle change occurs. Sex is ignored. No discussion, no innuendo, no nothing. This gradually leads into the correct attitude to be displayed in middle life, namely that sex is disgusting, when the same types of expression used to describe homosexual activity are in order (see previous).

Middle aged UMINI women should give the impression that sex is dirty, they are not interested in it and have never had it. This

8

Derling, et es purfectly raight end proper for you to merry

attitude is hard to sustain if a large family has been produced, but is necessary for the image. In the past an interesting way round the dilemma was offered by mothers to daughters on the brink of matrimony through the following advice. "Derling, et es purfectly raight end proper for you to merry. Relph es a gud boy. He hes ei fortune. But derling, doh yew know thet men cen be herd to setisfy? Yew must doh your best. Bai yourself a pair of long white gloves end ef he wonts yew to touch enything not quaite naice yew cen put them on."

Sales of long white gloves have plummeted so it is safe to presume this advice is either ignored or not given, but the point is still valid. Older women should subtly suggest that any sexual experience in the past was a matter of self sacrifice which thankfully is no longer necessary. Remarks such as "May Normen es a purfect gentlemen. He never leys ei finger on may" are in order.

The upwardly mobile gentleman of, shall we say, a certain age, has a sly attitude to sex. A difference between his expressed attitudes and his actions develop. He appears to agree with his wife. Of course he never lays a finger, or anything else, on his unwilling spouse. He is too tired because of the attention he pays to a dolly bird. As long as he manages to lead a double life

9

keeping his activities hidden from his wife and her friends his peers will nod approvingly and say, "Old Normen es ei bit of a led. He cen still put et ebout!" If he is caught two options are open to him. He can either scandalise his wife and her friends by setting up house with his dolly bird and enjoy the envy encountered when he appears in public with a beautiful bit of stuff on his arm, or he can repent of his wicked ways and plead for forgiveness.

Unfortunately the first option is available only for the seriously rich because of the claims the wife will have for maintenance, share of the value of the family home and because of the expense of legal fees.

Politicians in high office have only one option, which is also the only one open to the less seriously rich. Make peace with the wife. Express regret, sorrow, undying love, anything to save the marriage. Make sure she understands the financial implications of divorce. Make statements like "Derling Ay do not know whet ceme over me! How could Ay hurt the love of may life? Of course Ay will give you your share of the house end mentenence ef yew cen't forgive. Et is the least Ay cen do efter may bed beheviour. Solicitors cost en orm end ei leg, which of course would come out of the estate. The house is worth… end on ei good year Ay earn…, so you would hev… Yew would be poor, but Ay'm sure yew would hev enough money to bai a small house in en unfeshioneble district end Ay'm sure yew could menege. Yew could probably get a job. Ay het to think of yew heving to work. Pleese derling, forgive me."

Elderly UMINI women have high principles with over-riding priorities, namely they must always appear wealthy, live in a fashionable neighbourhood and not feel the need to work. The chances are 'Normen' will be forgiven, provided he convinces his wife that divorce on reasonable terms will cause her to be comparatively destitute.

Having saved his marriage 'Normen' should resign from all high office, look apologetic, proclaim he has made a simple human error. He and his wife should make as many public appearances as possible. This is the time to flash new clothes, jewellery etc. It is vital for both members of the partnership to look and sound uninterested in sex. Public displays of affection such as hand holding and fond glances are in order, but everything else is out. The correct attitude to be conveyed is that an errant hormone lingered in the male and is now thankfully cured. He should do his best to give the impression that he has recovered from a life threatening disease.

The subject of conversation is of vital importance to UMINIS. Ordinary mortals in Norn Iron talk about the weather. That is acceptable. It is unlikely to give offence and can be used as an

We hed a wee dence

introduction to a more impressive subject, such as, "Terrible weather whur heving, isn't it? Ay'm so gled Naigel end Ay meneged to teke a little breke in the Behemems. The weathur wos purfect. May deah, et wos just ei dream. Et wos quaite romentic. We drenk ei bottle of Sheto Nuv De Pep, thet's wayne you know, every night with ur dinner. May Naigel is quaite ei connosser of wayne. Et mede him quaite effectionete. Efter dinner we hed ei wee dence! The bend whur mervellous. They pleyed ell the old romentic numbers. Et quaite took me beck til ur courtin' deys."

The price of gold is another safe subject for conversations as is anything to do with the world of finance. Statements such as "Et tuk six months to recover from Bleck Mondey. Then we mede up ur losses bai purchesing some shures thet rocketed. One hundred thousend pound wus ei lot to lose!"

Every UMINI woman worth her salt will be heavily involved in raising money for charity. Often the aim is not so much to raise funds for those in need as to prove capable of spending money. To this end events are organised with tickets sold at extortionate prices. Money is frequently spent on organising the event rather than going to the needy. The result is that 'pore people' are unable to attend so the function is 'select' and suitable for UMINIS 'to be seen' at, and a pleasing self–sacrificing glow is felt while enjoying the pleasures of eating caviar and drinking champagne to help the world's unfortunates. Discussion of events organised for charity is suitable UMINI behaviour.

It is easy to 'talk proper' provided the basic ground rules are observed, no swearing, no discussion about homosexuality or sex, once the age of thirty has been attained, and ideally restrict the subject of conversations to exotic holiday locations, the price of gold, raising money for charity, finance and profits on property deals.

CHRISTMAS IN CHERRYVELLY

by Billy Simpson

"Hello Sendra. Is thet you Sendra? It's your sister Egnes. I'm just ringing to invite you and Semi over on the Seterday before Christmas for a wee sherry and a bit of semon petty. No weer not heving the big porty this year just a few friends. Hairy says now he's retired from earning money it's time Ay retired from spending it.

"Ay told him he can't take it with him when he goes but he just glures at me. Says for from taking it with him, the way ay spend it, he may have to leave early. End he wasn't leffing. Hairy can be very hord to live with since he retired. He's a right old cross petch sometimes. When he found out what ay paid for a teddy burr for the wee grandchild. Y'know Simon, Victorr's youngest, the one whats going to be an orchitect? Well, Hairy saw this receipt and went med. Said I could have bought a real burr for thet. I said a real burr would tear wee Simon till pieces. End do you know whit Hairy said? He said it would serve the wee git right for putting superglue in our video – the Penosonic one, y'know with the burr code thingy.

I said 'Hairold Johnston, I said. Is a Penosonic video more important than your own grendchild?' Hairy said Simon was a spoilt wee brat thet needed his erse skelpted. Honestly!

"He was just the same when I held thet wee cocktail porty for the sterving Efricans. When he got the bill for the elcohol and

13

vole-U-vonts he said it would have been cheaper to flay to Efrica and give them all a vole-U-vont each.

"Ay told him he was getting so mean, the Ghost of Christmas Pest would be efter him. He snepped beck thet the Ghost of Christmas Pest haunts him every Jenuary when he gets his benk statement. You hiv till leff.

"Ay don't know whit's got into may Hairy. When he was menaging the fectory he was as heppy as a lork. I hordly ever saw him. Now he's home he gets very sneppy about bills. But sure if ay didn't get may wee dender round Enderson end McAuleys every day, life wouldn't be worth livin, would it?

"Did your Semi get crebbit when he retired? No. Well ay suppose its a bit different in Bellybean. Thur's not the executive stress among the pore people.

"Enyway, do you know your Ent Elizabeth is coming over from Keneda this Christmas. Yes the one with the three husbands end all of thim dead. I don't know whit she does till thim. She was always a shameless woman fer the men you know. During the wor she had more Yenks thin Eisenhower. They used to call her Bleck-Out-Betty. Yeass. They said she could trip a Yenk and be under him before he hit the ground.

"Well now are you and Semi able to come on on the Seterday? Good. Well could you bring your old gremophone over when you come. A spring his gone on our radiogremme and they stopped making ports for it in 1948.

"Ay bought one of thim CD thingys but ay don't know how to work it. I tried to play may Dickie Velantine record and ay couldn't get it open to get the record intil it at all, even using the screwdriver. What? Oh yes ay still hev all Dickie's old records. Every time ay hear "All The Time End Everywhurr" aim jist enreptured.

"Y'know I think thet's whit attracted me to Hairy. He looked a bit like Dickie Velentine in those days. Except for the bold patch

14

and the big ears. They don't hev singers like Dickie any more. Not as clean. I saw thet MC Hemmer on the Tele the other day end you wouldn't COMPURR thim.

"Enyway bring your gremophone and your Net King Coles end we'll hev a wee Christmas dence. Oh. End if you are bringing wine again this Christmas, could you get a bottle this time and not one of thim cardboard boxes with the wee teps. Hev till go now. Murry Christmas Sendra".

You'll be able to pess yourselves off as a better kless of person

15

DENCING IN THE DORK

by Billy Simpson

"Hello. Is thet you Sendra? Its your sister Egnes from Cherryvelly. You sound breathless. What hev you been doing? Niver mind. I'm ringing to see if your electricity is off?

"Its a total bleckout here, end we were wondering if your Semi could bring us over a wee flesk of hot woter for a cup of tea. Oh! Bellybean is blecked out too.

"I know. Its epsolutely skendelous. If I'd known a wee storm could bleck out the country I'd never hev got Hairy to buy thim NIE shures.

"What? Oh! You and Semi went till bed to keep worm. Thets why you're out of breath? Oh! OH! Sendra really!

"No Hairy and I hev not gone till bed. We're sitting here surrounded by more kendles then the Veticen. We've been hevin' a wee gless of Sheto Nuve De Pep. Thet's wayne you know. From a bottle. Not thet stuff you buy in a box with a wee tep.

"Ectually its been quate romentic. We put on the radio end they were playing Net King Cole records, so Hairy and me were hevin' a wee dence. Hee Hee Hee. Yeaasss.

"Dencing in the dork,
"Till the tune ends,
"Wur dencing in the dork"

"Ay think the wayne was going till Hairy's head. He got quate effectionate. It took me beck till the Queen's Hop in the 1950s. Thet's whur I met Hairy. He was stending by the bendstend end he looked just like Deekie Velentine except for the bold petch and the big ears.

"Oh you're right, it was Denis Lotus. Deekie was the fet one. Enyway we didn't dence for very long. There was this wild epperition appeared at the French windows, teppin to be let in. It was thet Veronicer from next door. You know, the widow with the blonde rinse. Well, she came in and plenked herself down between me and Hairy on the sofa and said she was too fraytoned to stay on her own in the dork.

"Thet one fraytoned?!! Her thet broke thet man's leg at the Jenuary sales. Thet'll be the day.

"Enyway she was all over may Hairy and he's so easy till get round when he's hed a few. He was leffing and telling her how young she looks.

She was all over may Hairy

17

'Oh' she siz, 'You are lucky thim lights are out or you'd see may lefter lines.'

"LEFTER LINES? The woman's got a face like a corduroy jecket. So I sez, sweet as you like, well if them's lefter lines, it must must hev been a helluva joke. You must hev been trepped in a lift with Frenk Corson.'

"Well she give this dray leff end a glure you could skate on. Drenk heff a bottle of may gin end went home in a huff. Thet Veronicer was always a bitch. She was chasing other men before poor Edgar was cold in his urn. She was always like thet. Remember we used to see her swenking around at the dences in Romenos yerrs ago. She was the same then. Ay remember well thet night she came till me afraid she'd got pregnant. She said 'Egnes, Ay don't know how it heppened. It must hiv been something in the air thet night.' Yeasss, Ay thought. Your legs by the sound of it.

"Enyway Sendra, I'll let you get beck till your bed. Hairy's laying beck here on the sofa soun' till the world. When he wakes up with all these kendles round him, he'll think he's died if I'm not thur till let him see he's not in heaven yet".

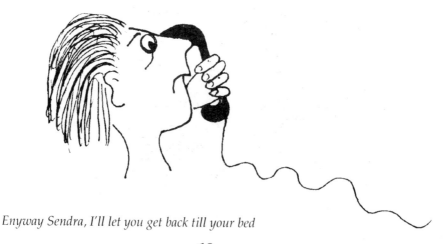

Enyway Sendra, I'll let you get back till your bed

THE LEND WE BELONG TILL IS GREND

by Billy Simpson

"Sendra. Is thet you? Oh thenk God you're home. Veronicer and Ay are epsolutely traumatised. You'll never believe whit heppened at the Cherryvelly Dremetic Society tonight.

"Whit heppened? You might well esk? Veronicer is here with me. She daren't go home in the state she's in. She's on teblets that don't mix with gin. At least not with a quart of it.

"But whit a night we hev hed. We were et rehearsals for the Dremetic Society's Christmas Concert. We're not doing a pento this yerr. Instead its going to be a tribute to the music of Roger Hemmerstein.

"Who? Rogers and Hemmerstein. Oh. They're two cheps are they? Well, its whoever wrote 'South Pacific'. Enyway, Veronicer and Ay were stending in the chorus heppily singing away at Oklahomo…

"We know we belong till the lend.
End the lend we belong till is grend."

"Suddenly this new young director they've hired fer the show jumps up and screams 'STOP! STOP! STOP THE MUSIC.'

"Veronicer and Ay were mystified because it sounded grend till us. Next thing he pointed right et us and esk the two of us till come to the front of the stage.

"Yiss," I said. "Whit is it Mr Director?"

"What do you think you are doing?" he said, all sercestic like.

"How do you mean?" I says. (Veronicer didn't say anything because her teblets were storting till fight with the gin she'd hed earlier.)

"That hand jive thing?" he said.

"Oh you mean holding our fingers in the air and swinging our heads from side till side?" Ay said. "We saw thet et a Berry Menelow concert, only they did it with kendles. We thought it would edd till the presentation."

"He shook his head and said thet we were supposed till be rough, tough frontier cowgirls not Berry Menelow groupies.

"You must be robust and YIP and slap your thighs when you sing this song", he says.

"Slep wur thighs?" I said. "But we don't slep wur thighs in Cherryvelly. Thets whit Germans do. We didn't even slep wur thighs when we did 'The Sound of Music' end thur wur Netzies in thet."

"He gives us a funny look and says, "Really," he says. "Well why are the pair of you are dressed like gipsy fortune tellers?"

"We are NOT gipsy fortune tellers," Ay told him, "These ur serongs. We dressed like this because we thought we were going till be singing 'Belly High' from 'South Pacific'. We thought it would edd till the tropical etmosphere."

"This is when he threw his head intil his hends and said there was no such song as 'Belly High'.

"Yis there is," I said. "The one the big fet woman sings till the sailors...

"*Belly High will call you*
Eny night or day
Belly High dah de dah de dah".

"Thet one," I said, thinking pore Roger Hemmerstein must be turning in his grave.

"Well! He slepped this clip board down on the chair and it

Belly High will call you, Eny night or day

crecked like a pistol shot. We all jumped beck.

"Its not Belly High," he shouted. "Its BALI HI! BALI HI! BALI...BALI...BALI. Come on say it. BAAA-LI HI. BAAAA–LI."

"Thets not the South Pacific," I said. "Thets more like East Entrim."

"He went all cold, efter I said thet. He glurred et me and said in one of thim voices you could cut a Veda with... "What does the word Belly mean to you?"

"Well netturally Ay said... "SWAN LAKE."

"Well he went epsolutely beserk. Rentin end raven like a THING possessed. Threw his clip board et the pianist and screamed something about working with cretins. Aren't thim the wee furry things in thet Steven Spielberg picture?

21

"Enyway by this time Ay was beside myself with rage. This young out-of-work theatrical coming till Cherryvelly with his page-boy hurrcut and talking till Veronicer and me like thet in front of everybody. Efter all the years Ay've given till the Orts in Cherryvelly. If it wasn't for may Hairy paying fer the costumes they've hev hed till hev done 'Ennie Get Your Gun' in thur shifts.

"And Sendra you know ay hev always been very ortistic. Remember Ay played the lead in 'The Berrets of Wimpole Street' et Eshliegh.

"Whit? Elizabeth Browning? No No. NOT her. Ay was Mr. Berrett. Remember efterwords the Dremer Critic of the 'Northern Whig' said Charles Laughton wasn't a petch on me when it came till frightening an audience. Ay still hiv thet cutting somewhere. Ah heppy days.

"Enyway, thet wasn't the worst of it. Ay grebbed Veronicer and led her beck till the dressing room and swore thet when Ay saw medim chairman of the Dremetic Society thet young upstort would be sent pecking.

"Ay couldn't wait till get out of thet serong end thet bleck make-up. The more Ay thought of us stending there singing Oklahomo dressed like slave girls, the defter ay felt. It was Veronicer's idea. Ay should niver hiv listened till her. She just wanted till wear thet revealing two-piece thet shows her navel. End Ay should niver hiv let her talk me intil puting on thet bleck make-up. It won't wash off! We've tried everything from shempoo till Flesh Liquid end it won't shift. When Ay took off may serong Ay looked like a Penda but Veronicer looks like a pedestrian crossing".

PROPER DRESS

by Doreen McBride

Keeping up appearances is of vital importance to the upwardly mobile in Norn Iron. It is impossible to join a group without appearing to be a member. A little bluff may be necessary. James Young, that late lamented Norn Iron personality had the right idea when he talked about women who saved money to buy a fur coat by doing without underclothing, referring to such individuals as 'the fur coat and no knicker brigade', or 'lace curtains and no sheets on the bed'. The point is outward appearances count while private details should remain private. If an object is not going to be prominently displayed UMINIS see no point in having it.

Ay feel very guilty when Ay wear this coat

Economise, do without and put the money into something flashy.

Today, fortunately for the upwardly mobile female, fur coats are no longer a requirement. Naturally if one has acquired a mink one should wear it on every conceivable occasion. If this is the case either of the following statements conveys the correct UMINI attitude.

23

(i)   "Conservetion? Ay think thet is ei lot of cod's wellop!
        This coat wes very expensive. Buying et wes sheer
        endulgence end Ay just love et. Ay jest decided Ay
        deserved ei little treat. End ef Ay could fend ai leperd skin
        coat Ay'd buy thet too!"

or

(ii)   "Of course Ay believe in conservetion deah! Ay really
        feel very guilty when Ay wear this coat. Ay would nevah
        bai ei new fur coat. This belonged to may deah old
        grenny. The dear little animals hev been dead ei long time
        end Ay do not like to think they daid in vein. Ay wear this
        coat out of sheer sentiment."

Older UMINIS are essentially very conservative. Their
attitudes linger from the past when few people had the opportunity
to be upwardly mobile because of grinding poverty. Most people
had only one set of clothes which was worn day in and day out.
The introduction of better working conditions led to the purchase
of a second set of clothes. Dress for workers was strictly regulated
so a set of clothes which differed from working ones was regarded
as a status symbol. During working hours men had to wear dark
suits, white shirts and black shoes so for leisure they bought
brown suits, blue shirts and brown shoes. Many a man was very
proud of his brown shoes!

The shape of the suit jacket became of vital importance. In the
past buildings were under heated and the majority of people
travelled to work by public transport so warm clothes were
essential. Most men's suits had four buttons then three became
common. In general the more buttons on a suit the shorter the
lapels and the warmer it was because more chest was covered
and not exposed to the elements. In the fifties and sixties men
could subtly imply they were either macho and did not feel the
cold or that they lived, in what was then, the rare comfort of
central heating and had a car, by choosing a suit with two, or even

one, button on the jacket instead of the more usual three. Today most offices and homes are centrally heated so the number of buttons on a suit jacket is unimportant. However the basic principle is still true. Upwardly mobile men must have an expensive looking business suit with hand stitched lapels to be worn with black shoes and preferably a fashionable tie. They also need expensive looking leisure clothes so that a virtue may be made out of looking casual.

In the past women also had to dress sensibly for work so frivolous working clothes were a status symbol. The female UMINI'S one desire in life was to marry well and escape the parental home. Local dance halls were a popular means of meeting the opposite sex so attire suitable for dancing was essential as were dancing lessons.

The upper crust attended Fosters at the corner of Malone Avenue on the Lisburn Road while lesser mortals went to Betty Staffs and John Dossers. Weekly 'hops' were held in Inst., Cavehill Bowling Club, Queen's University Union and Bostock House for the UMINI who generally avoided The Plaza (in Chichester Street), Betty Staffs, and John Dossers. The Floral Hall, The Orpheus and The Fiesta were unusual in that they were frequented by all types. UMINIS recognised unsuitable partners by the cheapness of their attire, their accent and language. Any girl invited to dance who replied, "Yew fff arf! Ah'm swatin'! Awa dance wi ma sister!" was clearly undesirable. Similarly any girl confronted by a boy saying, "Hallo snake! Will yew glide?" knew to reply "Ay would be delighted but Ay need to be excused," and then scuttle off and hide in the ladies cloakroom until a suitable length of time had elapsed, emerge, rejoin her friends and they would all look at the offending male and giggle so he knew to avoid them.

In the fifties leisure dress for women was eneveloped to ridiculous lengths. Full skirts were held out by hooped petticoats and layers of net underskirts so that they stuck out at waist level.

Today the same principles hold. UMINI women must wear sensible, good quality working clothes and possess a suitable supply of leisure clothes. Today's attitude is much more relaxed than that of the past so there is not as much scope for display. The void has been filled by the introduction of cheap clothes such as jeans and track suits with conspicuous designer labels and high price tags.

The old dance halls have gone, replaced by new 'hops' and discos. Greater freedom has evolved. Girls no longer risk being wall flowers. They are free to ask boys to dance, to gyrate by themselves or with girl friends. Dancing lessons are no longer de rigour, all that is necessary is the ability to throw the arms about and move the feet, preferrably in time to the beat, but as bodies no longer touch a sense of rythmn is not essential. If a girl is attracted by a boy she no longer has to entice him into asking her to dance. She can simply go up to him, wiggle in front of him in time to the music and shout, "What do you do?" The correct reply for males is "Ay'm en eccountent", (or student, or any professional occupation). The girl should reply "Ay'm ai lewyer", (or student or any other professional occupation). End Ay'm wif you!"

There are still unfashionable places. Generally speaking, anywhere connected with a University tends to attract the 'right type'. Pubs and bars tend to go in and out of fashion like yo-yos so young UMINI may need to do a bit of market research.

As far a older UMINIS are concerned, it is always correct to be expensively dressed although, in Belfast, the death of the old high status shops such as 'Robinson and Cleaver', 'Brands and Norman' and 'Anderson and McAuley' is to be regretted. If a garment is admired it is no longer possible to sigh, "Thenk you. Ay bought this little dress in 'Brends end Normens'." It is necessary to substitute an expensive make for the shop and say, "Thenk you. This is ei little Mondi number. Ay fends nothing fits me es well es Mondi."

Any UMINI woman worth her salt will appear in a constantly changing supply of designer clothes. This is not as difficult as would seem. Charity shops should be scoured for garments possessing designer labels. Labels frequently outlast the clothes in which they are sewn so may be carefully removed and replaced in a cheaper garment. It is also possible to remove a label from a position in which it is unlikely to be seen such as inside a dress and sew it into a jacket, coat or throw where it may be displayed while hanging casually over a chair. Better class designer label clothes may be bought from good quality, second hand clothes shops.

Always save the bags in which designer clothes are wrapped when bought new. These bags are invaluable when purchasing from less conventional outlets. Weigh the bag with a small item such as a pullover and carry it into the charity or second hand shop. The bag will serve a dual purpose. It may be used to carry any purchase home and it will show that you buy expensive items.

If spotted by an acquaintance inside a charity shop proclaim loudly, "Naice to see yew derling! Don't yew just love the wonderful cords, (or any other small item on display) one cen bai in here? Ay elweys support cherity. One should be kend to the less fortunet."

If caught inside a good quality secondhand clothes shop giggle in a slightly guilty, confused way and say, "Please don't tell may husband yew sew may! Ay hev bin so extrevegent! He'll jest dai if he fends out. Ay decided to sell some of may old clothes to defrey the bill!" This has two virtues. It shows an extraordinary amount of money has been spent and demonstrates that the cast off clothes are of sufficently good quality to raise money. Always remember that anyone found in an unconventional retail outlet is in all probability there for the same reason as youself. Show your breeding, act with confidence and keep up appearances.

Obviously the ideal situation is to be able to afford as many designer clothes as desired, to intimidate shop assistants by proclaiming in ringing tones "Thes es faine, but do you not heve enything more expensive?" Ignore common local sayings such as, "Those who are three pence short of a shilling know how to charge threepence more than a shilling."

Jewellry is essential to UMINIS. Just remember "All that glitters does not have to be gold". Gold and silver are always hall marked, usually in an unobtrusive fashion. Acquaintances are unlikely to insist on inspecting the marks so rolled gold and silver plate are entirely suitable. As far as UMINIS are concerned the value is comparatively unimportant, the look vital. Think of the success of a certain down market firm until the owner suggested it was selling good looking rubbish.

Quantity, not quality, counts. UMINIS should wear at least six gold chains of various designs. Add a couple of 'gold' bracelets and a couple of rings on at least two fingers of each hand. If money is a problem become a tuppence halfpenny swank.

Second hand jewellry is a good buy. There is no purchase tax on it so a bigger gem is available for less money.

Regarding jewellry, quantity counts

Gem size is everything. Auctions, junk shops and small out of the way antique shops are good sources of reasonably priced jewellry.

Antique jewellry generally is a good idea because it retains its value so can be sold if necessary. Also carefully used it gives the impression of a wealthy family background. If anyone admires a particular piece say something suitable in a modest fashion such as "May deah old grenny left may thet," or "May Enty

Sendra willed thet to me." Just remember, if you tell a lie it is vital to be consistent. I remember my dear old granny nearly laughing her leg off because an aquaintance attributed her ring to her 'old grenny' one day and her 'ent' a week later. Granny knew for a fact that the 'old grenny' in question had died in the work house! Of course with the introduction of unemployment benefit, old age pensions and state welfare and the passage of time such a faux pas is no longer possible, nevertheless it is still possible to make serious mistakes so UMINIS need good memories.

It is always a good idea to mount coins with a recognisable value, such as kruggerands and gold soverigns, on 'gold' chains and hang them around the neck. Miniature gold bars with large hall marks are also a good idea.

If somone admires the jewellry of a UMINI female she should look modest, bat her eyelids and claim it was a gift from her husband, boyfriend or partner. Say something like, "May Naigel bought may this for may birthdey." Never mind if Nigel would as soon fly in the air as buy jewellry and you got it yourself. Simply train him not to contradict and the gain high status given to UMINIS with friends prepared to splash out when buying a present.

Needless to say, if Nigel, or whoever, does happen to cough up an acceptable item reward him in any way which appears fitting. Make a big fuss. Go into orgasms of delight. Make sure he understands he has done something wonderful. Given sufficient reward he will probably repeat the action.

Male UMINIS do not have the same opportunity for display as females. However, a thick gold wedding ring, a good looking wrist watch and, when dressed casually, a heavy 'gold' chain around the neck always looks impressive.

Presentation of self is vital to UMINIS and it is worth going to a lot of trouble to convey the correct image. Remember, it does not have to be good as long as it looks good.

GORDON PARTY
AT THE KESSEL

by Billy Simpson

"It's me. Yer sister Egnes from Cherryvelly. Jist ringing till tell you about may day out et the Royal Gordon Porty et Hillsboro kessel.

"Yeaass. Moi end Hairy got invited but it wiz a secret. We couldn't even tell you and Semi. It was an epsolutely perfect efternoon, except for the rain, the mud and me het blowing away. We hid till park miles away fer security reasons and they took us to the kessel in a bus.

"End you know me end buses? I couldn't get on a Citybus without two vellium end a wee gin. But this was different. None of the riff-reff thet looks like they're used till buses.

"In fect everybody looked like they'd niver seen a bus in thur lives before. We were all stending thurr in our big flowered hets waiting for the driver till lower a remp or something but he told us we hed till get on without it.

"When we got till the kessel this big security gord tried till search me. I told him there wus no need because me end Hairy were from Cherryvelly, but he sid it didn't metter if we were from the Sen Fernendo Velly, we hed till be searched.

"Well, who wus the first one I bumped intill? VERONICER!

"Yeasss! Her from next door. Stending there enjoyin' being searched by this big gord. She hed walked pest the woman searcher end up till this tall chep with a big betton end insisted he ren his hends over her.

"Why thet hussy wis invited to a Royal Gordon Porty I kint understend? I know why me end Hairy were invited. Its all may yerrs of secrifice fer cherity. All thim coffee porties for the poor sterving blecks in Efrica. Lest winter Ay put on heff a stone with all the vol-u-vonts end kinnepes Ay hed till devour for the Etheopians alone.

"Enyway Ay was trying till avoid Veronicer and stepped intil this mud in me new shoes. By the time we got till the strawberry tent Ay was klebber till the knees. Then some ejit in a red helicopter nearly lended on top of us end sent may het flaying.

"Ay could hiv wept. End it wasn't even Princess Dienna who turned up. It was some Duke or somebody. Ay don't even know if he's related till the Royal Femily. Some wee slip of a lad brought may het beck. I was going till give a tip but somebody said he was a Minister for something et the NIO. But Ay kin't keep treck of these Government cheps. Just when you stort till recognise one, he gets forgiven end whipped beck to Lunding.

"We ren intil Veronicer looking for the drinks tent. Ay told her therr wus no drinks tent. It was only strawberrys end cream. Like Wimbledon. She went off in a huff. Probably till get a flesk out of her gorter.

"You know, Ay think thet woman is an elcoholic. At home you niver see her without a gless in her hend. End who could forget thet Kerr-O-Bean cruise?

"Remember her end Edgar came with Hairy end me to Jamaker. She got herself invited till the Keptain's table and then drenk herself under it.

"Then when we got till Jamaker she turned up et the pool porty et the hotel in one of thim string bikinis thet hed only a bit of cord for a beck. Ay tell you it was the biggest parcel thet string hed ever been tied round. Ay didn't know whur till look.

"Ay told her till her face thet she was a disgrace till Cherryvelly. And she jist leffed. Leffed!! Like ther was something funny about Cherryvelly?

"Till tell you the truth Ay don't think she could hiv been from Cherryvelly originally. She was niver our kind of person. There was something of the gipsy about her. More like somebody from somewhur like Bengorr.

"Enyway the eposlutely worst thing she did in Jamaker was the night she pulled up her skirt end storted to limbo under this stick when there already wus a big heff neked bleck man limboing through from the other direction.

"Well!! Thenk God her poor husband Edgar was beck on the ship in a Becardi coma end wasn't there till witness thet spectacle when Veronicer end thet big bleck chep met in the middle. It was epsolutely indecent.

"If it hed been Cherryvelly instead of Jamaker somebody would hiv thrown a bucket of water over thim".

At the gordon party

32

THE CHEERYVELLY ECEDEMY OF SPEECH AND DRAMER

by Billy Simpson

"Hello Sendra. It's me. Yer sister Egnes from Cherryvelly. Tell you whit I'm ringing about. Remember thet big het I lent youse for Gledys McCorkill's wedding. The big bleck one that Deddy said made you look like Barney Eastwood.

"Whit?? Oh Clint Eastwood was it? Ur they not the same person? Ay thought thet ector in "Dirty Hairy" became a boxing meneger efter he lost his looks.

"Oh they're two different people? Well you live end learn don't you.

"Enyway I need the het beck for Winsday efternoon. Its the only one thet goes with may new shoes. I'm not supposed to tell you this but your big sister hiz been appointed to the Board of Governors of Cherryvelly Ecedemy of Speech end Dramer.

"Yeaass. Its hord to believe efter all these yerrs. Its like a dream come true.

"Apparently it was a toss up between me end Gloria Hunniford but she's not one of the ecedemy's old girls you know. A lot of people think she is – but no. She niver came to our klesses. She's just a nettural.

"Netalie Bredshaw rang me lest night efter the governors emergency meeting. Apparently there wiz a big row end Medge Corter resigned in a huff.

You kin't call me a snob

"She sid the ecedemy was wasting its time in Cherryvelly because we already talk proper. She wanted till open the klesses to pore people.

"Lord knows, Sendra, you kin't call me a snob but we kin't hiv a lot of riff-reff coming in. Cor salesmen, radio personelities end thet.

"I expect they're not bed people but would you sit in a chair efter one of them? Ay think not. No ay think we should keep the Ecedemy as a centre of excellence for budding ectors and ectresses from Cherryvelly.

"But Netalie siz you couldn't reason with Medge Corter when she gets a bee in her bonnet. Netalie sid Medge stormed out saying she was off till Bellymena till set up her own speech klesses end do some missionary work.

"Well! Ay'll say this for Medge. She's not afraid of a chellenge. You heff till leff.

"Enyway the first meeting of the new Board is nixt Winsday end all the lady governors wear hets et the meetings. It's a bit like church without the collection.

34

"Oh thet reminds me Sendra, did youse know thet poor Clure Kemeron died suddenly? Remember, she wiz et Eshleigh with us? Big girl. Played goalkeeper fer the hockey team before she was expelled. You must remember her?

"Her second husband owned thet travel company thet sold time-shurs in Trensylvenia.

"Somebody said it was a skiing eccident. Poor Clure fell off the Metterhorn end they didn't find her for six months. Yeaass. But the snow kept her perfectly fresh for the funeral. Would you be without a freezer efter hearing thet?

"Her husband flew her beck till Belfast lest Setterday.

"I meant to go, but it was jist one of those days whin I wasn't in the mood for a funeral. Netelie and Medge were at it. They were supposed till sketter her eshes in the shoe department of Enderson end McAuley's but its shut now end when it opens again its going to hiv Mickey Mouse in it.

"Netelie didn't think Clure would hiv wanted till be trempted over by people dressed like big retts, so they jist skettered the eshes outside Yeegers".

ALL PORT OF LIFE'S RICH PETTERN

by Billy Simpson

"Hello Sendra, is thet you? Its your sister Egnes from Cherryvelly... Hello... Hello. Ur youse therr? I kint hear you... Heng on a minute. Ay'll tell Tarquin to turn down his hay-fi. Tarquin, Mummys on the phone so would youse mind torning thet recket down. There thet's better. Enyway Sendra ay wonder if you would maynd hiving mother for Christmas. Ay know, ay know, its may turn but she's draving us all med.

"Ay think Cheeryvelly is too hay-tech for mother. She'd be much heppier with you in Bellybean. Ay think she's pining for the sight of a jawbox again. May dishwasher is beyond her. Ay keep telling her everything in may house is autometic, but she keeps opening the front and pouring basins of water intil it. End she's been up with the garage door twice.

"But lest Seterday was the worrrst. She decided to hiv a beth so ay got her intil our Jerkuzi. Oh yes. Don't you hiv thim in Bellybean? You must come over for a dip sometime. No it doesn't hiv a diving board? Ur you being sercestic Sendra? Enywey the Jerkuzi was an epsolute disester. When the water started to bubble up round her she thought her old trouble hed come beck.

"She lept out of thurr like a scalded ket and ran out through our new conserve-a-tory intil the gordon. Epsolutely NECKET. Ay hid to tell the neighbours she was a stippergrem lukin for the rugby club.

She ran intil the gordon epsolutely NECKET

"End you know mother. You kint talk till 'er. She snepped the nose off me this morning when Ay told her Hairy and Ay are flaying to over to Lunding for Herrods sale. She sid Ay was all fur coat and no knickers.

"Efter all Ay've done fer thet woman! Enyway, the whole thing came till a head over the setelite television. Y'know we've got rid of thet big dish from the gordon. Hairy said it med the place look like a radorr station. We've got one of the little bleck one's now. Very discreet. You could hordly see it on our big roof.

"Alright. Don't snep at me Sendra, aim coming till thet. We were all sitting down watching Skay, it was a progromme with

Robin Day in it. You know. The crebbit one with the glesses. Well suddenly mother says 'Isn't he a bit old till be up in one of them things?' 'Whit things?' aye said. 'Thim setelite things,' she siz.

"Well I had till leff. 'Mother dear,' ay siz, 'Did youse think thet Robin Day was flaying round in space on the Storship Enterprise with Keptain Kirk?'

"So Ay explained it was only a wee ball in the sky and thet Robin Day was bounching his photo off it from Lunding.

"Who's up thurr driving it?," she siz. "Nobody's driving it," Ay siz. "It's autometic, like the dishwasher."

"WELL! She lets out this scream you could hiv heard in Bengorr. Then she got under the coffee table and sid thet if nobody wiz driving the setelite it could fall on our house. Honestly! She's med as a hetter.

"Enyway Hairy and Ay talked it over and we think she would be heppier with youse for Christmas. I mean your house his bin very low–tech since they repossessed your guess cooker. (CLICK.) …Hello. Sendra. Sendra… If youse hiv cut me off you'll niver see the inside of may split–level again, sister or no sister".

If nobody is driving the setelite it could fall on our house

THE YOUNG UMINI

by Doreen McBride

Today things have changed for young UMINIS. The situation is, in some ways, much more complicated than in the past. However, the over-riding principle remains the same. The young UMINI must give the impression of being loaded with money. Death duties and high levels of taxation have eroded inherited wealth and high unemployment has decimated the job market so the ability to obtain and hold down a job is a status symbol. This is the most obvious difference between past and present. Even Royals have obtained employment.

There are ways around the necessity of gainful employment, although they cannot, in all honesty, be recommended. There are those who have been in some way damaged by Norn Iron's troubles. These unfortunate individuals have the distinction of becoming UMINI sub-groups due to huge settlements being awarded by the courts as a result of compensation claims. This gives rise to NIOERs (Norn Iron Office claimants) and LIMPERS (knee cap victims).

During the fifties UMINI females took great pride in their parents' wealth. "Ay live in a big hus on the Melone Road", was the type of statement uttered with pride. As was "Ay don't need to work. Ay just stey et home end help Mummy." This had a double edged advantage in that it suggested the family was filthy rich and that the daughter was well schooled in household arts and was therefore qualified to make a good wife.

Upwardly mobile females did not have career prospects. They achieved status by making a suitable match, landing a partner who could support them in the style to which they were accustomed. Women with jobs were expected to leave on marriage and certainly after the birth of the first child.

Today young UMINIS need, as in the past, a car. A sports car is still awarded highest status but with high rates of insurance they are an impossible dream except for a fortunate few. A small new car is regarded as being without panache. Obtain a classic car such as an old Volkswagon beetle and have it restored.

Restoration of an old car will provide gainful occupation during periods of enforced unemployment. As in the past, it is not the reality which counts, but the image. Once suitable transport is obtained the young UMINI should not admit to do-it-yourself but should make statements such as "Ay wos so depressed when Ay wos mede redundent Deddy bought may ei cor."

A mobile telephone is another requirement. This need not be outrageously expensive. At present a suitable instrument may be hired for about £15 a month. That is really no more expensive than standard telephone charges and it rules out the need for an answer machine. It is vital to give the impression that one must be in touch at all times. However, there is a cardinal rule for mobile phones, NEVER ON ANY ACCOUNT, EXCEPT DIRE EMERGENCIES, MAKE OUTGOING CALLS. It is much too expensive. There are plenty of phones in quiet streets were outgoing calls and payment may be make, which dispenses with the shock of a telephone bill.

The best way for a young UMINI to appear prosperous is to live at home. Parents have a tendency to be soft hearted and will be satisfied if a nominal, if any, contribution is made towards household expenses. It is worth tolerating their foibles for the security, comfort, heat and food they supply. Also, peers may be just as unco-operative and difficult as parents without paying all of the rent.

Young UMINIS need a babe lair to entertain members of the opposite sex. It needs soft music, dim lights, plants, flowers and heat which is much easier to achieve in the parental home rather than in the crummy, cold, inexpensive accommodation that is usually all a young UMINI can afford.

Parental homes, with a little planning, may be used as babe lairs during periods of parental absence. Watch parents movements carefully. Find out when they are likely to go out and return.

Never completely deceive a parent. Lies have a habit of being discovered. Tell half truths. Say things such as "Do yew mend if Ay bring Cethoone oround to wotch ei video tomorrow night? She is a naice quaiet gurl. We would laike to see "Into the West". (Choose a decoy video title parents will recognise as harmless.) We missed thet show in the cineme end would reely laike to see it."

The request should be made for a night parents plan to be out. Hire the decoy, display it prominently. Keep any other ideas and videos hidden from view. Parents tend to be thick so it is possible to convice them that the intention is to watch things as naff as Disney cartoons. Do not think of this as deception. Remember you are doing them a favour as they can boast about their innocent and pleasant offspring who is unaffected by this terrible age of drugs, sex, alcohol, vice and violence.

The young UMINI

The situation should be explained to the friend. Explain the parents are going out and that company would be appreciated to watch a video.

The object of lust should be assessed cooly. Will he/she (in these days of sexual equality there is no reason why UMINI females should not attempt seduction) pass the parental eagle eye? Just remember parents do not appreciate grunge, long wild hair, ear-rings on men, transparent shirts or blouses, heavy make up or the type of clothes which would have caused my grandmother to make the following caustic comment, "What she hasn't got hanging out of that dress she's pointing at!" If you feel the object of your lust will pass the parents arrange for them to meet. Parents are less likely to rush home if they feel you are in the process of making the first moves to settle down into a suitable steady relationship. If a meeting with the parents appears unwise say something like "Rodnai (or Cethorone) is so sorry he (she) is wurking lete this evening. He (she) will not be eble to come round until efter you heve left. He (she) would love to meet yew."

If your partner in crime is likely to impress parents explain it would be a good idea to appear interested in a naff video until after the old foggies have gone and ask for suggestions for more suitable entertainment. Remember, some parents have bad memories and tend to forget things so give them plenty of time to clear before starting anything realy interesting. Then enjoy! Just remember what happened to Cinderella at mid-night, keep an eye on the clock and make sure you are not caught in an embarrassing position. You can always finish the session in your car before you take 'Cethorone' home.

Young UMINIS have inherited attitudes from their parents. The only basic difference is they are driven by youthful urges which require them to find a mate so are fascinated by sex while their parents are attempting to forget about IT.

WHEN HAIRY MET SELLY

by Billy Simpson

"Hello Sendra. Its me again. Your sister Egnes. Just reng to invite you over on Setterday evening. I'm heving a few of the old girls from Eshleigh over.

"Its sort of a combination bridge porty end a wee wake for poor Enderson end McAuley's closing.

"I know you couldn't afford to go intil it too often but its like a wee chepter of may life is over. When I think of all the heppy hours I spent in thure trayin' on shoes.

"Donegall Place won't be the same. They are nearly all gone now. The Benk Buildings, Robinson and Cleavers, Brends and Norman's. Enyway we'll be hevin' a wee sherry and a vol-U-vont on Setterday. End do you know who's going till be thur? – Elice Tettersall! Yeaass!

"The one thet ren off with thet Yenk who told her he hed a big kettle rench in Texas. Turned out to be a keravan in the desert, two pigs end a rettlesnake. You heff till leff.

"Remember she came beck and married thet orchitect from Bengorr and he died of a hort etteck teaching her till drive. They found thim on the roundabout. Him gesping for breath and her screamin' it wasn't her fault and it was a stupid place till put a brake enyway.

"Well, she's married again. Yeass. Some ex-Civil Servant end she gets till all the Royal Gordon Porties at Hillsboro Kessle end everything. End she's a turrible snob now according to her syster

Myrtle. Keeps a big photo of Princess Diena on the piano end pretends she knows her well. My dear she barely got witin wavin' distance of the woman niver mind a hendshake.

"Lest yerr she claimed she hid cauaght thet Royal disease, Bulimia Nervosy. If it was feshionable, Elice would ketch it. She storted going on eating binges but didn't think being seek efterwords was very dignified.

"She put on a stone and a heff. Oh we hed a leff about thet. Thur wasn't a dray seat in the house.

"When I think of whit she was like at Eshleigh. Men med she was. Thur wasn't a Kembell boy thet was safe in his blazer. Thet Elice Tettersall flettened a bit of gress in her time.

"End look at her now. A beckside like the Belmoral bus and a waist thet'll niver see the inside of a size 16 again. She's as fet as a butcher's ket.

"Whit's thet Sendra? Mother? Oh she's beck in the home. She didn't want till go but Ay explained thet it was for her own good. Because if she stayed with me a week longer Ay'd hev murdered her.

"The night before we took her beck, we were watching this film on television "When Hairy Met Selly". Well there was a very embarrassing scene in it at a resturant. Oh. You know the one.

"Well! When thet Meg Reyn storted moaning and grunting, mother went quate frentic. Storted shouting thet Meg Reyn hid got it wrong end began threshing about like an Efrican witch doctor. Ay hed till put my hend over her mouth and hold her down because young Tarquin wiz in the room at the time.

Young Targuin wiz in the room

PORDON, YOUR SLIP ES SHOWING

by Doreen McBride

I am eternally grateful to Egnes Hairiot Johnston for the afternoon she spent coaching me in the ways of UMINIS. I was allowed to stand on a piece of brown paper in front of her bed room mirror (she felt dandruff could fall out of my hair and contaminate her pristine carpet) and encouraged to practise the correct expression. Thanks to Egnes's generosity I now know how to hold my mouth as if I were about to begin whistling and how to speak with the correct accent through the small space in the center.

Egnes took time to impress upon me that prounciation is of vital importance to UMINIS. "It is quaite easy," she said, "provided yew remember to errenge yer mouth properly end tawk through the wee gep in the middle."

What UMINIS say is also important according to Egnes. It is all too easy to lapse into Norn Ironspeak. As Egnes explained, "Wur surrounded bai common people. It's turribly easy to slip into bed hebits. Low down people tawk about 'yer moer' end 'yer faer', or even worse, 'yer ma' end 'yer da' ". As Egnes said, "The ket hes ei 'moer' end ei 'faer', Ay know of no enemel which hes ei 'ma' ur ei 'da'. You shood sey 'may mother and may feyther' or 'Mummy end Deddy, of course may Tarquin colls may 'Mumsy'."

According to Egnes, an obvious slip is to refer to a partner as 'thole woman' or 'thole man', expressions which common Norn Iron speakers may also use to denote more mature individuals. The proper thing to say is 'may wife' or may husband' and never ever copy the TV. character who refers to his wife as 'er indoors' which translates locally as 'im upstairs' a derogatory expression used to refer to a husband with a tendency to be lazy.

Everyone in Norn Iron belongs to one of two religions. It is the nature of the Province. There are numerous stories of strangers being asked their to name the religion to which they subscribed. The questioner on hearing the stranger was a Buddhist (or any other 'foreign' religious sect) then asked "Well, are you a Protestont Buddhist or a Catholic Buddhist?" According to Egnes, UMINIS usually 'keep to thur own sort' but are willing to do business with anyone providing the opportunity for profit. If religion is mentioned talk about 'Kethlics end Protestonts' not 'Catholics and Pradestants', and remember "Yew must olweys wotch the other sort es yew cen't trust them — thur aies ur too close together".

Upwardly mobile people lunch in the middle of the day and have dinner at night. The more polite the society the later, within reason, the dinner. The ideal time is around 8 o'clock. This shows it has been necessary to work late at the office, earning thousands, if not millions, but still allows sufficient time for a reasonable life style. As Egnes explained, "May Hairy never errived in from wurk till well efter siven. He was sooooo busy meking money thet Ay could spend in shops laike Enderson end McAuley's."

If UMINIS become drunk they become maudlin or amorous or vomit in public but they never start a fight or become in any way argumentative. That is reckoned to be bad form. Egnes explained "Evun may friend Veronicer cen drink a gellon of gin

Drunk UMINIS never become argumentative in public

47

end not orgu. She may ect es if she's in heat but she'll not foll out with yew."

According to Egnes, it is considered indelicate to mention toilets. She says Norn Iron UMINIS have not as yet adopted the American custom of regarding the word 'toilet' as almost indecent. Americans replace the word 'toilet' with 'bathroom' and will ask to go to 'the bathroom' in places like railway stations, airports and streets where one would not normally expect to find a bath within miles, never mind a room in which to put it. 'Bethroom' is acceptable in Norn Iron as is 'cloakroom', 'little boys (or gurls) room' or 'Pleese would yew show may the geography of the house?' The more delicately necessary bodily functions are mentioned the more UMINI the individual. I said to Egnes "I suppose such expressions as 'Ah needa slash!' and 'Ah'm goin' to the bogs' are out?" and she fainted. When she recovered she suggested I leave the house immediately as she was suffering from her 'nurves'. However, she was kind enough to send me a list of essential rules for good behaviour which she asked me to "shure with the other pore pethetic people".

EGNES HAIRIOT JOHNSTON ESSENTIAL RULES

FOR GOOD BEHAVIOUR

1.   Meke money

2.   Hev money

3.   Spend money